WHITE SHROUD

BY ALLEN GINSBERG

Poetry

Collected Poems 1947–1980. 1984.

Howl and Other Poems. 1956.
Kaddish and Other Poems. 1961.
Empty Mirror, Early Poems. 1961.
Reality Sandwiches. 1963.
Angkor Wat. 1968.
Planet News. 1968.
Airplane Dreams. 1969.
The Gates of Wrath, Rhymed Poems 1948–51. 1972.
The Fall of America, Poems of These States. 1973.
Iron Horse. 1973.
First Blues. 1975.
Mind Breaths, Poems 1971–76. 1978.
Poems All Over the Place, Mostly '70s. 1978.
Plutonian Ode, Poems 1977–1980. 1982.

Prose

The Yage Letters (w/ William Burroughs). 1963.
Indian Journals. 1970.
Gay Sunshine Interview (w/ Allen Young). 1974.
Allen Verbatim: Lectures on Poetry, Politics, Consciousness (Gordon Ball,
     ed.). 1974.
Chicago Trial Testimony, 1975.
To Eberhart from Ginsberg. 1976.
Journals Early Fifties Early Sixties (Gordon Ball, ed.). 1977.
As Ever: Collected Correspondence Allen Ginsberg & Neal Cassady (Barry
     Gifford, ed.). 1977.
Composed on the Tongue (Literary Conversations 1967–1977). 1980.
Straight Hearts Delight, Love Poems and Selected Letters 1947–1980, w/
     Peter Orlovsky (Winston Leyland, ed.). 1980.
Howl, Original Draft Facsimile, Fully Annotated (Barry Miles, ed.). 1986.

ALLEN GINSBERG

WHITE SHROUD

POEMS

1980-1985

"Old lovers yet may have
All that Time denied—
Grave is heaped on grave,
That they be satisfied—"

HARPER & ROW, PUBLISHERS, New York

Cambridge, Philadelphia, San Francisco, Washington
London, Mexico City, São Paulo, Singapore, Sydney

Thanks to hospitable editors, variants of these writings were printed first in: *Action, American Poetry Review, Apartment, Art contre/against Apartheid, The Atlantic, Big Scream, Bombay Gin, Christopher Street, Folger Library Broadside, Full Circle, Here Now, Hidrogenski Dzuboke, L. A. Weekly, Long Shot, Mag City, Nagyvilag, NAMBLA Journal, Naropa Institute Bulletin, National Lampoon, New Age, New Blood, Northern Literary Quarterly, Open, Paris Review, Partisan Review, Peace or Perish, Poesi 1 (Oslo), Poetry, Poetry East, Portable Lower East Side, riverrun, Spao Spassiba, Sulfur, The New York Times Magazine, Tribu, United Press International, Vajradhatu Sun, Vanity Fair, White Shroud (Kunsthalle, Basle).*

FIRST EDITION

Designer: Sidney Feinberg

Library of Congress Cataloging-in-Publication Data
Ginsberg, Allen, 1926–
  White shroud.
  Includes indexes.
  I. Title.
PS3513.I74W46 1986   811'.54   86-45104
ISBN 0-06-015714-3   86 87 88 89 90 HC 10 9 8 7 6 5 4 3 2 1
ISBN 0-06-015715-1 (limited)

To
Edith Ginsberg

Contents

Acknowledgments

Steven Taylor: Lead sheets; Walter Taylor: Lyric calligraphy.

Harry Smith: Archetype design for cover, executed by Julie Metz.

Bill Morgan, Bob Rosenthal, Juanita Lieberman, Gary Allen and Vicki Stanbury helped assemble typescript texts.

Aaron Asher & Terry Karten, Editors; Marge Horvitz, Copy Editor; Bill Monroe, Surveyor of Detail.

WHITE SHROUD

Porch Scribbles

Balmy, hotter outside than in the living room—
        Wind rustles the rattlesnake reeds.
Didja see the Perseus star shower last night?

        *   *   *

Bright on Flatirons, sunshine gleams
        on clouds, on brown shake shingles,
                tree limbs rock,
So bright on the car roof, I gotta sleep—

        *   *   *

I want that brick house on Mapleton,
it's for sale "Moore Real Estate"—
        But price too high,
I'm too drowsy to go to the telephone.

        *   *   *

Clouds float up from the end of the world—
        Have we enough room for population explosion?
Call up Gary, let's find out what he thinks.
                          July 11, 1980

That tree stands higher than a house
        like a dog with hair drooping over its mouth—
green long beanpods hang from its branches

        *   *   *

It's a whale that big gray-bottom cloud floating
over the Flatirons, it's a mushroom, a shipcastle, a
        mountain with sunshine and Coasts—
                It's a pile of mist.

        *   *   *

Look up, clouds in the sky,
        suddenly their shadows fall where Mrs. Hurst
           on Mapleton Street sprays her front lawn.

        *   *   *

Midsummer, green leaves thick on maples
        The front yard, white flowers—
           Cause it's just so beautiful now!
How sad, to be alive watching the season at its height—

        *   *   *

Spray the lawn, it's too hot—
Street children call, car radios play muted disco
                Gray clouds umbrella brilliant sun
I used to be young once, bewildered
                like that barechested little
                        girl across the street.

                    *   *   *

Where I sit, leg over my knee
listening to the whippoorwill call of a distant ambulance,
the thin tree's little leaves startle and jump,
raindrops fall thicker & the smell of ozone
                wafts across the porch.

                    *   *   *

Everyone loves the rain, except those caught in their
                                business suits,
birds whistle, tree leaves shake excited, electric smells
rise across the City to the watchers on the balcony—

                                August 2, 1980

Did the Ecologist chop his girl with an ax in Philadelphia
                & hide her corpse a year in the trunk?
What does that red-haired boy half-naked on the sidewalk
                with his Frisbee think of that?

                                Boulder, August 3, 1980

Industrial Waves

Tune: *Capitol Air*

The New Right's a creepy pre-Fascist fad
Salute the flag & call on Mom & Dad
Shit on the niggers it's their fault they were slaves
In a free market you can get rich filling graves.

Freedom for the rich to suck off the Work of the Poor
Freedom for Monopoly to corner the market in horse manure
Freedom for the secret police and guys with guns
Freedom for bully buys! Death to the Radical Nuns!

Freedom to buy Judges! Freedom for organized crime!
Freedom for the Military! "I got mine."
Hundred millions free to starve, isn't that great?
Freedom for the Neutron bomb to radiate!

Freedom for War! Fight for Peace! Whoopee!
"Government off our backs"—except the Military!
Freedom for Narcs to put junkies in jail!
Freedom to punish sick addicts, all hail!

Freedom to bust you for grass if you please
Freedom to beat you up when you're down on your knees
Freedom for Capital Punishment, without fail!
Freedom to wiretap your phone & open up your mail.

Freedom for Causa Nostra's pornography
Freedom to ban your verse in the high school library
Freedom to stop deaf widows' food stamps
Freedom to draft-register everyone wearing pants.

Free computerized National Police!
Everybody got identity cards? At Ease!
Freedom for Big Business to eat up the sea
Freedom for Exxon to examine your pee!

Freedom of the air for William Buckley
Freedom for Mobil to buy up TV

Freedom to influence Network News
Freedom for money to make you wear shoes.

Freedom to fink out Nicaraguan liberty
Freedom to shove them into Soviet economy!
Freedom for Costa Rica to eat our military scenes
Freedom in Honduras for Contras & Marines!

Freedom for Indonesia to murder half million
Freedom for South Africa to stabilize the Bullion
Freedom for South Africa to slave her Blacks
Freedom for Korea's corrupt party hacks.

Freedom for America to kick plenty Ass
Allende Lumumba yass yass yass!
Freedom for Martin Luther King it's a gas
Freedom to forget our bloody Indochinese past!

Freedom to be Macho to be Number One
Freedom to boast the heaviest nuclear gun!
Freedom to kill for KKK
If you got a White Jury you might get away.

Freedom to work if you don't Unionize
Freedom to listen to Presidential lies
Freedom to have your name in Secret Service file
Freedom to run with the Mob for a while.

Freedom from government regulation!
Freedom to not be allowed an abortion!
Freedom for old folks to enjoy inflation
Freedom to destabilize the Chilean Nation!

Freedom to abandon Latin Human Rights
To deport John Lennon for his Political delights
Freedom to ban Genius entering the Land
& slap Nobel Prize novelists on the hand.

Freedom for overt Covert War sleaze
Freedom for Death Squads to chop off your knees
Freedom to put pederasts in Prison
Freedom to stop Fairies from eating Gyzym.

Freedom to assemble & get gassed or shot
Freedom to not be allowed to smoke pot
Freedom to drink till you got the DT's
Freedom to never take LSD.

Freedom to smoke & have your Utah Cancer
Freedom to shake down a bottomless Dancer
Freedom to be forbidden Peyote Vision
Freedom to censor *Howl* on Television.

Freedom to farm if you're a big bank
Freedom to go bankrupt or land in the tank
If you're a small farmer who grows a little grass
Freedom to be arrested & kicked in the ass.

Freedom to cut down world's oldest trees
Freedom to make Indians get down on their knees
And pray to your God and obey your FBI
And freedom to protest if you're not too scared to die.

Freedom to persecute the Underground Press
& Murder Malcolm X if that's what you think's best
Freedom to Assassinate, & never go to jail
If the CIA Protects you, and they hardly ever fail.

Freedom to squirt Mace in a little boy's face
If you're on the TAC Squad & you don't like his race
Freedom to shoot him if he makes you nervous
And he's 12 years old and you've just joined the service.

Freedom to bribe Japan if you're Lockheed
You won't go to jail unless you're smoking weed
Freedom to buy Iran if you want
At least we used to, right now we can't.

Freedom to foment a Strike in Chile
And lie to Congress if you're Pres. of ITT
Freedom to kill an elected President
If you're a CIA stringer, that's how it went.

Freedom to commit a little perjury—
If your name is Richard Helms, you pay a little fee

Then get yourself appointed Ambassador to Iran
They keep calling you Ambassador as long as they can.

Freedom to sell dope if you're CIA
Or a Narc on the Street you can do it anyway
Or the sister of the Shah or informer for the law—
If your name is Abbie Hoffman you might take a fall.

Freedom to announce what you want to the Press
They print what they hear, it's anybody's guess
The public is free not to hear what you meant
But there's freedom for full-page advertisement

If you're Mobil, if you're Dow, or a millionaire Jerk
Buy a column on the Op Ed page for your work
If you're rich as Rockefeller you can die without your pants
Sniffing poppers and the papers won't give yr corpse another glance.

If you're AT&T you have plenty Liberty
To wave your flag all over the land of the free
You can take the back page of The News in Review
To say what's good for America's nothing else but you.

If you got a million from a Texas millionaire
You can buy television time, get yrself on the air
Freedom to shut up if you're Powerful Poor
Freedom to wait outside the Police Station door.

You're free to denounce any Pinko that you please!
You can ask for Moral Money, give your God's heart ease!
Free to attack the producers in a rage
Free to land in Jail, get beat up on the back page.

Freedom to be one of the few that count
Freedom to be "Serious," that freedom'll amount
To the fact that you're free to agree to more Cold War—
Flakes & Losers are free to go 'way sore.

                                                March 1981

Those Two

That tree said
    I don't like that white car under me,
                it smells gasoline
That other tree next to it said
    O you're always complaining
        you're a neurotic
      you can see by the way you're bent over.

July 6, 1981, 8 P.M.

Homage Vajracarya

Now that Samurai bow & arrow, Sumi brush, teacup
& Emperor's fan are balanced in the hand
—What about a glass of water?
Holding my cock to pee, the Atlantic gushes out.
Sitting to eat, the Sun & the Moon fill my plate.

July 8, 1981

Why I Meditate

I sit because the Dadaists screamed on Mirror Street
I sit because the Surrealists ate angry pillows
I sit because the Imagists breathed calmly in Rutherford and Manhattan
I sit because 2400 years
I sit in America because Buddha saw a Corpse in Lumbini
I sit because the Yippies whooped up Chicago's teargas skies once
I sit because No because
I sit because I was unable to trace the Unborn back to the womb
I sit because it's easy
I sit because I get angry if I don't
I sit because they told me to
I sit because I read about it in the Funny Papers
I sit because I had a vision also dropped LSD
I sit because I don't know what else to do like Peter Orlovsky
I sit because after Lunacharsky got fired & Stalin gave Zhdanov a special
       tennis court I became a rootless cosmopolitan
I sit inside the shell of the old Me
I sit for world revolution
                 July 19, 1981

Love Comes

I lay down to rest
weary at best
of party life
& dancing nights
Alone, Prepared
all I dared
bed & oil
bath, small toil
to clean my feet
place my slippers neat.

Alone, despair—
lighthearted, bare-
bottom trudged about,
listening the shout
of students down below
rock rolling fast and slow
shaking ash for show,
or love, or joy
hairless girl and boy
goldenhaired goy.

The door creaked loud
far from the crowd
Upstairs he trod
Eros or some god
come to visit,
Washed in the bath
calm as death
patient took a shit
approached me clean
naked serene

I sat on his thighs
looked in his eyes
I touched his hair

Bare body there
head to foot
big man root
I kissed his chest
Came down from above
I took in his rod
he pushed and shoved
That felt best

My behind in his groin
his big boyish loin
stuck all the way in
That's how we began
Both knees on the bed
his head to my head
he shoved in again
I loved him then

I pushed back deep
Soon he wanted to sleep
He wanted to rest
my back to his chest
My rear went down
I rolled it around
He pushed to the bottom
Now I've got 'em
He took control
made the bed roll

I relaxed my inside
loosed the ring in my hide
Surrendered in time
whole body and mind
and heart at the sheet
He continued to beat
his meat in my meat,
held me around
my chest love-bound
sighed without sound

11   *Love Comes*

My breast relaxed
my belly a sack
my sphincter loosed
to his hard deep thrust
I clenched my gut tight
in full moon light
thru curtained window
for an hour or so
thin clouds in the sky
I watched pass by
sigh after sigh

He fucked me in the East
he fucked me in the West
he fucked me South
my cock in his mouth
he fucked me North
No sperm shot forth

He continued to love
I spread my knees
pushed apart by his
so that he could move
in and out at ease,
Knelt on the bed
pillow against my head
I wanted release

Tho' it hurt not much
a punishment such
as I asked to feel
back arched for the real
solid prick of control
a youth 19 years old
gave with deep grace,
body fair, curly gold
hair, angelic face

I'd waited a week
the promise he'd keep
if I trusted the truth
of his love in his youth
and I do love him—
tall body, pale skin
Hot heart within
open blue eyes—
a hard cock never lies.

July 4–October 11, 1981

Old Love Story

Some think the love of boys is wicked in the world, forlorn,
Character corrupting, worthy mankind's scorn
Or eyes that weep and breasts that ache for lovely youth
Have no mouth to speak for mankind's general truth
Nor hands to work manhood's fullest delight
Nor hearts to make old women smile day and night
Nor arms to warm young girls to dream of love
Nor thighs to satisfy thighs, nor breath men can approve—
Yet think back to the time our epic world was new
When Gilgamesh followed the shade of his friend Enkidu
Into Limbo's dust to talk love man to man
So younger David enamored of young Jonathan
Wrote songs that women and men still chant for calm
Century after century under evergreen or palm
A love writ so sacred on our Bible leaf
That heart-fire warms cold millennial grief.
Same time Akilleos won the war at Troy
Grieving Patroklos' body, his dead warrior boy
(One nation won the world by reading Greek for this
And fell when Wilde was gaoled for his Bellboy's kiss)
Marvelous Zeus himself took lightning eagle shape
Down-cheeked Ganymede enjoyed God's thick-winged rape
And lived a youth forever, forever as can be,
Serving his nectar to the bearded deity
The whole world knew the story, the world laughed in awe
That such Love could be the Thunder of immortal Law.
When Socrates climbed his ladder of love's degrees
He put his foot in silence on rough Alcibiades
Wise men still read Plato, whoever they are,
Plato whose love-lad Aster was his morning star
Plato whose love-lad was in death his star of Night
Which Shelley once witnessed as Eternal Light.
Catullus and tough Horace were slaves to glad young men
Loved them cursed them, always fell in love again
Caesar conquered the world, top Emperor Power
Lay soft on the breast of his soldier of the hour
Even Jesus Christ loved his young John most
Later he showed him the whole Heavenly Host
Old Rome approved a beautiful bodied youth

Antinöus Hadrian worshipped with Imperial Truth
Told in the calm gaze of his hundred stone
Statues standing figleafed in the Vatican.
Michelangelo lifted his young hand to smooth
The belly of his Bacchus a sixteen-year youth
Whose prick stands up he's drunk, his eyes gaze side-
Ways to his right hand held up shoulder high
Waving a cup of grape, smart kid, his nose is sharp,
His lips are new, slightly opened as if part-
Ed to take a sip of purple nakedness,
Taste Michelangelo's mortal-bearded kiss,
Or if a hair-hooved horny Satyr happens to pass
Fall to the ground on his strong little marble ass.
Michelangelo loved him! What young stud
Stood without trousers or shirt, maybe even did
What the creator wanted him to in bed
Lay still with the sculptor's hand cupped on his head
Feeling up his muscles, feeling down his bones
Palm down his back and thighs, touching his soft stones—
What kind of men were the Slaves he tied to his bed?
And who stood still for David naked foot to head?
But men love the muscles of David's abdomen
And come with their women to see him again and again.

Enough, I've stayed up all night with these boys
And all my life enjoyed their handsome joys
I came with many companions to this Dawn
Now I'm tired and must set my pen down
Reader, Hearer, this time Understand
How kind it is for man to love a man,
Old love and Present, future love the same
Hear and Read what love is without shame.

I want people to understand! They can! They can! They can!
So open your ears and hear the voice of the classical Band.

October 26, 1981

AIRPLANE BLUES

SLOW BLUES

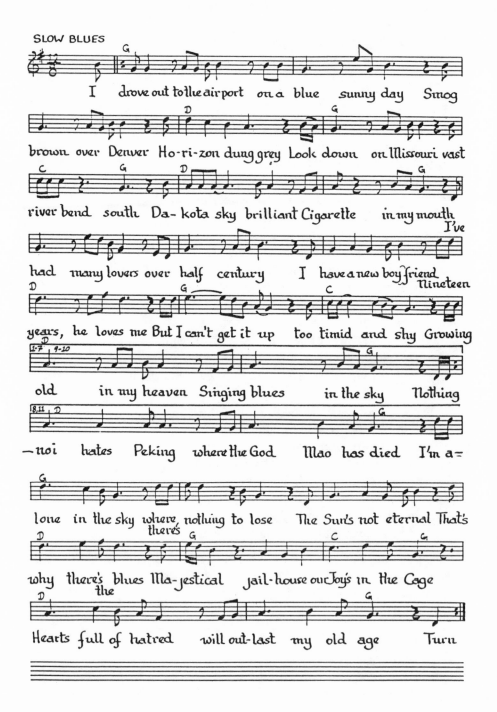

Airplane Blues

I drove out to the airport
                    on a blue sunny day
Smog brown over Denver
                    Horizon dung gray
Look down on Missouri
                    vast river bend south
Dakota sky brilliant
                    Cigarette in my mouth

I've had many lovers
                    over half century
I have a new boyfriend
                    Nineteen years, he loves me
But I can't get it up
                    too timid and shy
Growing old in my heaven
                    Singing blues in the sky

Nothing here to complain of
                    White clouds in the sun
Peace in my heart
                    Empty sky Everyone
But earth I look down on
                    Turns round misery
Green dollars fat
                    with the war industry

Mankind's great delusions
                    Scrape sky with red rage
Build bombs out of Atoms
                    to blast out the words on this page
Majestical jailhouse
                    our Joy's in the Cage
Hearts full of hatred
                    will outlast my old age

*   *   *

My mother has perished
                    my father's long dead
I have a sweet brother
                    healed the pain in his head
I'm going to the Apple
                    to eat with my friends
While the radio chatters
                    what the President intends

Down there Mississippi
                    Minneapolis near
Farms and green comforts
                    of the Northern Hemisphere
While Earth's hundred millions
                    Chew miserable clay
Old African kingdoms
                    Starve this century

I'll read in the papers
                    more deaths in Iran
Jahweh rules Israel
                    Tanks in Afghanistan
Martial Law rules Gdansk
                    and the old Viet-Nam War
Murders Indians in Guatemala
                    and burns down El Salvador

London and Belfast
                    Los Angeles and Prague
Tel Aviv & Moscow
                    sit in their smog
Phnom Penh's red ruin
                    was Washington's pride
Hanoi hates Peking
                    where the God Mao has died

I'm alone in the sky
                    where there's nothing to lose
The Sun's not eternal
                    That's why there's the blues
Majestical jailhouse
                    our Joy's in the Cage

Hearts full of hatred
>> will outlast my old age

* * *

Turn round in the sunset
>> over Manhattan isle
Newark was my birthplace
>> under the wing for a while
Green gastanks of Kearny
>> Smog brown in the sky
Seven million black men and white
>> live here and die

Come down over Harlem
>> red buildings stand still
Dusk light gleams their windows
>> wheels bound on the landfill
Sky streaked with jet streams
>> black clouds in the west
In the Lower East Side
>> I'll go take my rest.

October 30, 1981

DO THE MEDITATION ROCK

MODERATE SHUFFLE

If you want to learn how to me-di-tate I'll tell you now 'cause it's never too late I'll tell you how 'cause I can't wait it's just that great that its never too late If you are an old fraud like me or a lama who lives in E-ter-ni-ty The first thing you do when you me-di-tate is keep your spine your back-bone straight Sit yourself down on a pillow on the ground or sit in a chair if the ground isn't there if the ground isn't there if the ground isn't there sit where you are if the ground isn't there

Do the medita-tion Do the medita-tion Learn a little Patience and Gene-ro-si-ty

Do the Meditation Rock*

Tune: *I fought the Dharma, and the Dharma won*

If you want to learn	how to meditate
I'll tell you now	'cause it's never too late
I'll tell you how	'cause I can't wait
it's just that great	that it's never too late
If you are an old	fraud like me
or a lama who lives	in Eternity
The first thing you do	when you meditate
is keep your spine	your backbone straight
Sit yourself down	on a pillow on the ground
or sit in a chair	if the ground isn't there

    Do the meditation   *Do the meditation*
    Learn a little Patience and Generosity

Follow your breath out	open your eyes
and sit there steady	& sit there wise
Follow your breath right	outta your nose
follow it out	as far as it goes
Follow your breath	but don't hang on
to the thought of yr death	in old Saigon
Follow your breath	when thought forms rise
whatever you think	it's a big surprise

    Do the meditation   *Do the meditation*
    Learn a little Patience and Generosity
    Generosity   *Generosity*   *Generosity & Generosity*

All you got to do	is to imitate
you're sitting meditating	and you're never too late
when thoughts catch up	but your breath goes on
forget what you thought	about Uncle Don
Laurel Hardy Uncle Don	Charlie Chaplin Uncle Don
you don't have to drop	your nuclear bomb
If you see a vision come	say Hello Goodbye
play it dumb	with an empty eye
if you want a holocaust	you can recall your mind
it just went past	with the Western wind

    Do the meditation   *Do the meditation*
    Learn a little Patience   *& Generosity*

* Buddhist Samatha-Vipassana Sitting Practice of Meditation

If you see Apocalypse   in a long red car
or a flying saucer   sit where you are
If you feel a little bliss   don't worry about that
give your wife a kiss   when your tire goes flat
If you can't think straight   & you don't know who to call
it's never too late   to do nothing at all
Do the meditation   follow your breath
so your body & mind   get together for a rest
    Do the meditation   *Do the meditation*
    Learn a little Patience   *and Generosity*

If you sit for an hour   or a minute every day
you can tell the Superpower   to sit the same way
you can tell the Superpower   to watch and wait
& to stop & meditate   'cause it's never too late
    Do the meditation   *Do the meditation*
    Get yourself together   *lots of Energy*
    & Generosity   Generosity   *Generosity & Generosity!*

                                                St. Mark's Place, Xmas 1981

The Little Fish Devours the Big Fish

When the troops
get their poop
at Fort Bragg
how to frag
Sandinistas
Leftist Nicas
or go bomb
Guatemalan
Indians

Make a tomb
for men & boys
ending joys
of villages
and pillage
or burn down
to the ground
little huts
where pigs rut

This costs much
tax money as such
for an error
of red terror

Hypocrisy
is the key
to self defeating
prophecy

Genia Yevtushenko
Ernesto Cardenal
Allen Ginsberg
Rocknroll
sentimental
& reliable
& poetical
& prophetical
Therefore urge
Washington
& Havana men
to relax
& reflect
that the ax
on the neck
of Nicaragua's
a big error
of war fever

Double bind
makes us blind
to self fulfilling
prophecy—
If you're willing,
lose your eye
& your ear
mad with fear

Hypocrisy
is the key
to self fulfilling
prophecy

You can bet
Marxist threat
starts with that
self fulfilling
prophecy
if you're willing
to admit
that the threat
of invasion
of a nation
might cause them
great alarm,
Make them arm
to resist,
mobilize
to insist
they will fight
back all right—
Then to condemn
their armed men
and not molli-
fy their fears
is sheer folly
O my dears!

Hypocrisy
is the key
to self fulfilling
prophecy

United States
you're the greatest
Superdick
your big stick
& big mouth
North & South
causes fear—
Armies near
and armies far
or army talk
wherever you are
makes folks here

think you're queer
Big gun boats
that you float,
big rumors
that you dote
on will be quot-
ed in Managua
Santiago
Buenos Aires
& Havana
as more dread
threat of war
and Central
America will
Mobilize
militarize
and devise
a defense,

it's common sense.
Then to complain
that their plan
to fight back
is a pain in the neck
of the Pentagon—
Washington
is crazy, Man.

Hypocrisy
is the key
to self fulfilling
prophecy—
If you're willing—
costs an eye
and an ear
mad with fear.
Intercontinental Hotel Bar, Managua
January 25, 1982, 11 P.M.

Happening Now?

Happening now? End of Earth? Apocalypse days?
President says "Armageddon!" $254 Billion Military Budget!
The 5 A.M. subway train leaves Times Square
Crowded with murderers & corpses sitting in dress suits,
Earphones listening to mechanical disco, infinite
Deaf universe of Walkman   Happening now
While I drink Perrier at parties in Bel Air
Neutron bomb Nerve Bacteria gas, fruit fly recombinant
Germ plasm, Stratospheric X-ray laser
Anti-rocket beams, MX Cruise Stealth & Pershing missiles
In dream ten years ago I stood on a South Texas crossroad
Walked out alone from what City I couldn't remember
Half the sky was covered with ink-black cloud
Tanks and bombers moved toward the distant horizon

February 7, 1982

A Public Poetry

The fact is, the Russians are sissies
And Chinese big yellow sissies too
Americans by their nature sissies
Ran away to the New World & beat up Indians,
Now we're gonna let Peabody Coal take their Four Corners away!
So sissy we exploded Atom Bombs on Japs!

I myself a famous sissy, it takes one to know one
and know State Secretary XYZ a prissy sissy
Gave his nickels to Indian killer Juntas in Guatemala
Too freaked out to look El Salvador Deathsquads in the eye
Yelling tiny Nicaragua's a big threat to undernourished Mexico!
President ABC's the biggest sissy
Hollywood sissy
Bechtel Corporation sissy
Such a sissy he gave 200 Billion Dollars to Pentagon Bullies
frightened they'll beat him up if he don't let the Generals grab all his
    money
And the American public's sissy too
Scared if they don't give everything in their pockets to Defense
    Department
the muscle men at the Pentagon and tough guys at CIA'll
beat up Congress and Supreme Court
and take over the whole Western Block.

April 6, 1982, 2:00 P.M.

"What You Up To?"

"Oh just hanging around
        picking my nose . . ."
I replied, embarrassed
        in Naropa's corridor,
the Sanskrit professor'd saluted me
as Americans are wont to do—
What must he think my genius,
        a large red blob on my
        index finger tip—
But I suffer from Bell's palsy
my lower eyelid slightly paralyzed
no longer conducts tears thru
        my nostril
thus my nose corridors dry up
        & crack, for five years
whenever I lift the handkerchief
        from my face
a spot of red stains the pure
        cotton & shames me.
When I walk with bent spine & cane
        will my nose be caked with
blood black & ulcerous? tears
        running down my cheeks
a bony pinkie picking at the
        scarlet scab that got thick
overnight, I forgot to grease my
        wrinkled snout the nite
        of my eightieth birthday

and dreamed all the red
        mountain of mucus accumulated
        round me
Himalaya of suffering gelatinous
        slop my lifetime since 1976
when the right side my face
        drooped dead muscles
'cause an O.D. on Doctor's Antibiotic
        inflamed my seventh cranial nerve inside
        its cheekbone

& left me dry-nosed with crooked
      smile & sneaky finger
Probing the irritation in the
      middle of my face
walking daydreaming in the school hall—
That White boy in a two-piece suit
      Hotel Astor bar on Times Square
I took home one night in 1946
      he fucked me naked in the ass
till I smelled brown excrement
      staining his cock
& tried to get up from bed to go to the
      toilet a minute
but he held me down & kept pumping
      at me, serious & said
"No I don't want to stop I like it dirty
      like this."

April 30, 1982

Maturity

Young I drank beer & vomited green bile
Older drank wine vomited blood red
Now I vomit air
                July 1982

"Throw Out the Yellow Journalists of Bad Grammar & Terrible Manner"

for Anne Waldman

who report Ten Commandments & Golden Rule forgetting *Thou shalt
not bear false witness Do unto others as you'd have them do
unto you*
and say the Man got crucified for insulting the Sanhedrin at a Victory
Dance in the bombed out madhouse in Beirut
Out! Out! The Mad Correspondent who headlined "Madman or Messiah?
He Died of Bad Pork" the night of Tathagata's Parinirvana
or the snide reporter with yellow teeth who asked the Big Question,
"Kerouac couldn't write, so what'd he do it for, money?"
or the *Time* stringer who asks "You could say it was a nostalgia Trip,
wouldn't you?"
as you fly off to the moon on your translucent sexual wings forever
and the wire-service fellow ex-Harvard, "This business about Secret
Police, why would you care, successful Abstract Expressionist
painter, got a grudge to work out on your parents?"
Out! Out! into the Buddhafields, among stars to wander forever, weight-
less without a headline, without thought, without newspapers
to read by the light of the Galaxies.

August 10, 1982

GOING TO THE WORLD OF THE DEAD

Jews Let Go   Let Go Let Go   Let Go Israel   Ho Ho Ho Let

Go A-pocalypse Go Let Go   Let go Yr Bomb   Ho Ho Ho Your
         Let

Going to the World of the Dead

Going to the World of the Dead
Stalin & Hitler in Bed
Gone inside of your head
Anybody got any bread?
FBI papers to shred?
Eisenhower's ghost on a sled
Going to the world of the dead
Everybody gives you good head

Millionaires of Detroit
Millionaires of Chicago
Millionaires of New York
Millionaires of Hollywood
Let go of your money Ho Ho Ho
Let go your Big Poetry Let go Let go

Let go of your cars   Ho   Ho   Ho
Let go your Cocaine   Ho   Ho   Ho
Let go your meat Let go Let go
Let go Movie Picture Ho   Ho   Ho
Let go your Diamonds   Ho   Ho   Ho
Let go your Dollars Let go yr Gold

Let go your Houses Your Bodies Let go
Let go your Souls   Ho   Ho   Ho
Let go God   Buddha Let go
Let go Allah   Let go Let go
Let go your Armies   Ho   Ho   Ho
Let go your war   Ho   Ho   Ho

Let go your Holy   Land Let go
Let go Palestine   P.L.O.
Jews Let go Let go Let go
Let go Israel   Ho   Ho   Ho
Let go Apocalypse Let go Let go
Let go Yr Bomb   Ho   Ho   Ho

Your Nuclear Bomb   Ho   Ho   Ho
Let go your Disaster your Death Let go
Ho   Ho   Ho   Ho   Ho   Ho
Ho   Ho   Ho   Ho   Ho   Ho
Millionaires of Mexico   Ho   Ho   Ho
Millionaires of Nicaragua Let go Let go

August 22, 1982, 6:30 P.M.

*Guasave–Las Mochis bus past soya & cotton fields where red flags flew over
plastic huts squatting by highway side*

Irritable Vegetable

Don't send me letters   Don't send me poems
Too busy sick to write poetry   Sky's covered with gray clouds
Perfect for photography
I have brain metal fatigue   Knee jerk aesthetic tears
So you got a junk habit
So you need a recommendation to Purgatory U.
So you're working with Fort Collins' Nuclear Freeze Campaign
So you got hi blood pressure   Your big toe hurts
Someday you'll die
So you sing Hare Krishna Hare Krishna Krishna Krishna Hare Hare
        Hare Rama Hare Rama Rama Rama Hare Hare
So you work on the top floor of the Empire State Building
You're a jerk
You're a hypocrite who eats hot dogs.
October 28, 1982

Thoughts Sitting Breathing II

When I sat in my bedroom for devotions, meditations & prayers
my Gomden on a sheepskin rug beside the mirrored closet,
white curtains morning sunlit, Friday *Rocky Mountain News* "Market
  Retreats in Busiest Day"
lying on the table by Nuclear Nightmare issue of *Newsweek*,
Katherine Mansfield's thick bio & Addington Symonds' *The Greek Poets*
lifting a white lamp above my headboard pillow illuminating *Living
  Country Blues*' small print 1 A.M. last night,
with B complex bottled, green mint massage oil, High Blood Pressure
  nightly Clonadine Hydrochloric pills,
athlete's foot Tolnaftate cream, newsclip scissors and a rusty shoe-last
  bookweight standing on xeroxed Flying Saucer papers,
new ballpoint pens, watch, wallet, loose coins keys Swiss army knife
toothpicks, pencil sharpener & filefolder of Buddhist Analytic Psyche
  papers
scattered random across this bedstead desk—
As I breathed between white walls, Front Range cliffs resting in the sky
  outside south windows
I remembered last night's television suitcoat tie debate, the neat Jewish
  right wing student outwitted a nervous Dartmouth pimply
  liberal editor
knowing that boy who swears to "get the Government off our backs"
  would give my tax money to Army brass bands FBI rather
  than St. Mark's Poetry Project—
He can't read verse with any sense of humor sharp eyed
but then some poets can't either, did Ed Dorn find me fatuous, can I
  breathe in hot black anger & breathe out white cool bliss?
Doomed guilty layman all my life! these pills causing impotency?
Could I move bookcases & clothes out of my bedroom, 8 foot desk file
  cabinets & typewriter
to the small apartment next door N.Y., would that end my hideous Public
  Karma,
Telephones tingling down my spine, pederast paranoid hypnotic burnt
  out teenage fruitcake poets
banging the door for protection from Brain Damaged Electric Guitar
  Police in New Wave Blue Vibration Uniforms?
Be that as it may as blue empty Buddha floats through blue bodied sky,
should I settle down & practice meditation, care for my nervous Self, do
  nothing,

arrange paper manuscripts, die in Lower East Side peace instead of heart
     attack in Ethiopia,
What way out of this Ego? let it appear disappear, mental images
Nothing but thoughts, how solve World Problems by worrying in my
     bedroom?—
Still one clear word-mighty poem might reveal what Duncan named
     Grief in America
that one hundred million folk malnourish the globe while Civic Powers
     inflate $200 billion War Machines this year—
and who gets rich on that, don't all of us get poor heart?—but what do
     I know of Military Worlds?
Airfields and Aircraft Carriers, bugle Corps, ice cream concessions,
million dollar Computer rockets—yes I glimpse CIA's spooky dope deal
     vanity—but nothing of Camp Pendleton's brainy Thoughts
Norfolk officers' vast housing tracts, messes and helicopters, food re-
     source
logistics Pentagon committees've amassed—NORAD's Rapture Moun-
     tain
Maybe get rid of Cold War, give Russian Empire warm weather access,
inaugurate trillion dollar Solar Power factories on every Continent—
Yes access to sunny blue ocean, not Cold Murmansk & Vladivostok Ports
     they need a vast hot harbor
International Agreement big warships forbidden, no battleships from
     Russia or America in the azure Greek pond—
What about pirates, storms at sea or kamikaze Hell's Angel North
     Africans shooting Jews?
Well a few small Police boats, no Cruisers or Nuclear Subs—
Yes a warm weather port for Russian access South I thought
sitting on my bedroom floor cushion 10:30 A.M. getting hungry breath-
     ing thru shades & curtains on transparent windows, morning
     sun shining on white painted walls and gray rug—
So remembering the old story of Russia's claim to a warm weather harbor
     I came back to myself, blue clouded Colorado sky adrift above
     the Bluff Street Boulder house.

                                                    November 8, 1982

What the Sea Throws Up at Vlissingen

for Simon Vinkenoog

Plastic & cellophane, milk cartons & yogurt containers, blue & orange
    shopping bag nets
Clementine peels, paper sacks, feathers & kelp, bricks & sticks,
succulent green leaves & pine tips, waterbottles, plywood and tobacco
    pouches
Coffee jartops, milkbottle caps, rice bags, blue rope, an old brown shoe,
    an onion skin
Concrete chunks white pebbled, sea biscuits, detergent squeezers, bark
    and boards, a whisk-brush, a box top
Formula A Dismantling Spray-can, a whole small brown onion, a yellow
    cup
A boy with two canes walking the shore, a dead gull, a blue running shoe,
a shopping bag handle, lemon half, celery bunch, a cloth net—
Cork bottletop, grapefruit, rubber glove, wet firework tubes,
masses of iron-brown-tinted seaweed along the high water mark near the
    sea wall,
a plastic car fender, green helmet broken in half, giant hemp rope knot,
    tree trunk stripped of bark,
a wooden stake, a bucket, myriad plastic bottles, pasta Zara pack,
a long gray plastic oildrum, bandage roll, glass bottle, tin can, Christmas
    pine tree
a rusty iron pipe, me and my peepee.

January 3, 1983

I Am Not

I'm not a lesbian screaming in the basement strapped to a leather
        spiderweb
I'm not a Rockefeller heart attacked in the paramour bed with pants off
I'm not a radical Stalinist intellectual fairy
not an antisemitic Rabbi with black hat white beard & dirty fingernails
not the San Francisco jail cell poet beaten by minions of yellow police
        New Year's eve
not Gregory Corso Orpheus Maudit of these States
nor yet a schoolteacher with marvelous salary
I'm not anyone I know
in fact I'm only here for 80 years

St. Clement's Church, March 7, 1983

I'm a Prisoner of Allen Ginsberg

Who is this Slave Master makes
      me answer letters in his name
Write poetry year after year, keep up
      appearances
This egotist whose file cabinets
      leave no room for more
      pictures of Me?
How escape his clutches, his public sound,
      bank accounts, Master Charge
      interest
Who's this politician hypnotized my life
      with his favors
Petty friends & covert Nemesis, dead heroes and
      living ghosts hanging around
waiting Genius handout?
Why's this guy oblige me to sit
      meditating,
shine rocknroll Moon on Midwest Collegetown
      stages blind in overhead
      spotlights
bawling out of tune into giant microphones
makes me go down suck teenage boys
I declare a new life, how can I pay all
      his debts
next month's rent on his body,
      bald & panicky, with Pyronie's disease
Cartilage stuff grown an inch inside
      his cock root,
non-malignant.
           Karme-Choling, April 4, 1983, 12:15 A.M.

221 Syllables at Rocky Mountain Dharma Center

Headless husk legs wrapped round a grass spear, an old bee trembles in sunlight.

Since yesterday noon two Brown-eyed Susans stand before the outhouse door.

Tail turned to red sunset high on a spruce crown one lone chickadee tweets.

Moonless thunder—yellow dandelions flash in fields of rainy grass.

Mad at Oryoki in the shrine-room—Thistles blossomed late afternoon.

Put on my shirt and took it off in the sun walking the path to lunch.

A dandelion seed floats above the marsh grass with the mosquitos.

Empty clouds drift above me, birds chirp, a plane roar falls down through blue sky.

Electric noon—pine bough cicadas buzz outside the machineshop door.

At 4 A.M. the two middleaged men sleeping together hold hands.

In the half-light of dawn a few birds warble under the Pleiades.

Sky reddens behind fir trees as larks twitter and sparrows cheep cheep cheep.

July 1983

Caught shoplifting ran out the department store at sunrise and woke up.

August 1983

Fighting Phantoms Fighting Phantoms

Fighting phantoms we have car wrecks on Hollywood Freeway
Fighting phantoms th'Egyptians mummified Pharaohs & rich businessmen
Fighting phantoms a young Scotsman wore tennis shoes on the battleship
    deck
Fighting phantoms William S. Burroughs wrote umpteen novels
Fighting giant phantoms David picked up his sling
Fighting phantoms Chögyam Trungpa Vidyadara founded Shambhala
    Kingdom
Fighting phantoms pay federal taxes few write tax refusal forms
Fighting phantoms a Son of God ascended his wooden cross
Fighting summer phantoms muscular young musicians jumped up scream-
    ing in the twilit movie theater
Fighting phantoms Siddhartha meditated under a Bo tree
Fighting phantoms mysticism entered into the Catholic Church of
    Hollywood
Fighting phantoms a hundred thousand kids ordered purple Mohawks
Fighting phantoms various fairies chased adolescent athletes through
    steam bath locker rooms
Fighting phantoms the ruling class blew up the military budget, 244 Bil-
    lion dollars 1985—of the tax pie 63% if past military debt interest
    & pensions're added in
Fighting phantoms Ronald Reagan sent cocaine armadas to Central
    America
Fighting phantoms poets who smoked cigarettes denounced cigarettes—
Fighting phantoms New York Times printed thousands of editorial pages
Fighting phantoms Adolf Hitler shot more Methamphetamine & chewed
    the Bunker rug
Fighting phantoms thousands of poets become rather good at acid satire
Fighting phantoms Jimmy Dean stepped on the gas, Orson Welles or-
    dered another cheesecake
Fighting phantoms Ernest Hemingway shotgunned his brain
Fighting phantoms Ezra Pound hated some Jews some hated Pound
Fighting phantoms Truman dropped two Atom Bombs
Fighting phantoms Einstein invented the theory of relativity

Mid-August 1983

Arguments

I'm sick of arguments
"You threw the butter in the pan"
"I did not you let it melt on the stove"
"You invaded Turkey and killed all the Armenians!"
"I did not! You invaded China got them addicted to Opium!"
"You built a bigger H Bomb than I did"
"You used poison gas in Indochina"
"Your agent orange defoliated ¼ the landmass   It isn't fair"
"You sprayed Paraquat"
"You smoke pot"
"You're under arrest"
"I declare war!"
Why don't we turn off the loudspeakers?
                                    September 5, 1983

Sunday Prayer

An itch in the auditory canal scratches for years, use unguent,
Back pain a little, turn my head neck hurts
Balding long ago, gray whiskey hair inside ears
Eyes closed lying in bed, smart on my tongue, delicate
raw gums sore round some tooth roots—
From nineteenth year College chronic active Hepatitis
affects my kidney stones & high-blood pressure
Right cheek paralyzed slightly, eye squints tired,
lethargy dumps, no one's abdomen to kiss,
cock skewed and lumpy erection aches—
Why show myself these sicknesses? Show anyone?
Wisdom & senescence, sickness and Death come
legended from Buddha to Kerouac—Myself
suddenly older—I made a mistake long ago.

September 25, 1983

Brown Rice Quatrains

Those high lunches needn't matter
If you're of businessman's age
Anyway he enjoyed creating food
drifting across the Fragrant Nation

Who was it that began mouth talk
Gave the citizens thoughtful Saliva
Nature boy came close to Government
but secret police maintained ham & eggs

What tragedy for multiple Chickens
Think how pigs dream butcher night!
Sheep squawked nightmare, goat
fish sent regrets from meadow and sea

If he only could've made new Congress
We wouldn't breathe so much sulfur smog
Sugar dances at the movies, coffee tells you on TV
and Sodium Nitrate & Nicotine Cholesterol

have nothing to do with Foreign policy.
Nature boy drifts into Central American oblivion
with Seminole Patchwork and Albert Einstein,
nobody thought heat rays would end the world.

September 25, 1983

They're All Phantoms of My Imagining

I needed a young musician take off his pants sit down on the bed and
        sing me the blues
I needed a teacher could nail me to the Unborn
needed a stepmother'd accomplish my natural mother's tears
a scared friend of fame wearing locks and T'fillin by the Wall of Tears
I needed a brother was gentle, suffered to protect me from anger
needed a nephew lost, left his rice in the refrigerator with a cold spoon
Comrade farmer cook with me & study Banjo Dharma
Needed Presidents mad so I could write the Nation sane
I needed a father a poet would die
Needed the great companion dark eyes wearied brow tender heart in the
        grave
needed an intelligent junkie rebuke my shallow thought with dirty wit
an old girlfriend take my picture, give me a bed—
A college to be kicked out Columbia
scandal jail the clang of Iron madhouse to wake my 22'd year
Invented all these companions, wept & prayed them into flesh
needed these Creatures to be Allen Ginsberg this my self
crying the world awake mid oceans of suffering blood
needed to be the liar of Existence in America
Manslaughter showed me the True Falsehood of Law
Needed a Buddha enlightened I be enlightened
a bed to sleep in, a grave to cover my ashes.

October 1, 1983

White Shroud

I am summoned from my bed
To the Great City of the Dead
Where I have no house or home
But in dreams may sometime roam
Looking for my ancient room
A feeling in my heart of doom,
Where Grandmother aged lies
In her couch of later days
And my mother saner than I
Laughs and cries She's still alive.

I found myself again in the Great Eastern Metropolis,
wandering under Elevated Transport's iron struts—
many-windowed apartments walled the crowded Bronx road-way
under old theater roofs, masses of poor women shopping
in black shawls past candy store news stands, children skipped beside
grandfathers bent tottering on their canes. I'd descended
to this same street from blackened subways Sundays long ago,
tea and lox with my aunt and dentist cousin when I was ten.
The living pacifist David Dellinger walked at my right side,
he'd driven from Vermont to visit Catholic Worker
Tivoli Farm, we rode up North Manhattan in his car,
relieved the U.S. wars were over in the newspaper,
Television's frenzied dance of dots & shadows calmed—Now
older than our shouts and banners, we explored brick avenues
we lived in to find new residences, rent loft offices
or roomy apartments, retire our eyes & ears & thoughts.
Surprised, I passed the open Chamber where my Russian Jewish
Grandmother lay in her bed and sighed eating a little Chicken
soup or borscht, potato latkes, crumbs on her blankets, talking
Yiddish, complaining solitude abandoned in Old Folks House.
I realized I could find a place to sleep in the neighborhood, what
relief, the family together again, first time in decades!—
Now vigorous Middle aged I climbed hillside streets in West Bronx
looking for my own hot-water furnished flat to settle in,
close to visit my grandmother, read Sunday newspapers
in vast glassy Cafeterias, smoke over pencils & paper,
poetry desk, happy with books father'd left in the attic,
peaceful encyclopedia and a radio in the kitchen.

An old black janitor swept the gutter, street dogs sniffed red hydrants,
nurses pushed baby carriages past silent house fronts.
Anxious I be settled with money in my own place before
nightfall, I wandered tenement embankments overlooking
the pillared subway trestles by the bridge crossing Bronx River.
How like Paris or Budapest suburbs, far from Centrum
Left Bank junky doorstep tragedy intellectual fights
in restaurant bars, where a spry old lady carried her
Century Universal View camera to record Works
Progress Administration newspaper metropolis
double-decker buses in September sun near Broadway El,
skyscraper roofs upreared ten thousand office windows shining
electric-lit above tiny taxis street lamp'd in Mid-town
avenues' late-afternoon darkness the day before Christmas,
Herald Square crowds thronged past traffic lights July noon to lunch
Shop under Macy's department store awnings for dry goods
pause with satchels at Frankfurter counters wearing stylish straw
hats of the decade, mankind thriving in their solitudes in shoes.
But I'd strayed too long amused in the picture cavalcade,
Where was I living? I remembered looking for a house
& eating in apartment kitchens, bookshelf decades ago, Aunt
Rose's illness, an appendix operation, teeth braces,
one afternoon fitting eyeglasses first time, combing wet hair
back on my skull, young awkward looking in the high school mirror
photograph. The Dead look for a home, but here I was still alive.
            I walked past a niche between buildings with tin canopy
shelter from cold rain warmed by hot exhaust from subway gratings,
beneath which engines throbbed with pleasant quiet drone.
A shopping-bag lady lived in the side alley on a mattress,
her wooden bed above the pavement, many blankets and sheets,
Pots, pans, and plates beside her, fan, electric stove by the wall.
She looked desolate, white haired, but strong enough to cook and stare.
Passersby ignored her buildingside hovel many years,
a few businessmen stopped to speak, or give her bread or yogurt.
Sometimes she disappeared into state hospital back wards,
but now'd returned to her homely alleyway, sharp eyed, old
Cranky hair, half paralyzed, complaining angry as I passed.
I was horrified a little, who'd take care of such a woman,
familiar, half-neglected on her street except she'd weathered
many snows stubborn alone in her motheaten rabbit-fur hat.
She had tooth troubles, teeth too old, ground down like horse molars—
she opened her mouth to display her gorge—how can she live

with that, how eat I thought, mushroom-like gray-white horseshoe of
incisors she chomped with, hard flat flowers ranged around her gums.
Then I recognized she was my mother, Naomi, habiting
this old city-edge corner, older than I knew her before
her life diappeared. What are you doing here? I asked, amazed
she recognized me still, astounded to see her sitting up
on her own, chin raised to greet me mocking "I'm living alone,
you all abandoned me, I'm a great woman, I came here
by myself, I wanted to live, now I'm too old to take care
of myself, I don't care, what are you doing here?" I
was looking for a house, I thought, she has one, in poor
Bronx, needs someone to help her shop and cook, needs her children now,
I'm her younger son, walked past her alleyway by accident,
but here she is survived, sleeping at night awake on that
wooden platform. Has she an extra room? I noticed her cave
adjoined an apartment door, unpainted basement storeroom
facing her shelter in the building side. I could live here,
worst comes to worst, best place I'll find, near my mother in
our mortal life. My years of haunting continental city streets,
apartment dreams, old rooms I used to live in, still paid rent for,
key didn't work, locks changed, immigrant families occupied
my familiar hallway lodgings—I'd wandered downhill homeless
avenues, money lost, or'd come back to the flat—But couldn't
recognize my house in London, Paris, Bronx, by Columbia
library, downtown 8th Avenue near Chelsea Subway—
Those years unsettled—were over now, here I could live
forever, here have a home, with Naomi, at long last,
at long long last, my search was ended in this pleasant way,
time to care for her before death, long way to go yet,
lots of trouble her cantankerous habits, shameful blankets
near the street, tooth pots, dirty pans, half paralyzed irritable,
she needed my middle aged strength and worldly money knowledge,
housekeeping art. I can cook and write books for a living,
she'll not have to beg her medicine food, a new set of teeth
for company, won't yell at the world, I can afford a telephone,
after twenty-five years we could call up Aunt Edie in California,
I'll have a place to stay. "Best of all," I told Naomi
"Now don't get mad, you realize your old enemy Grandma's
still alive! She lives a couple blocks down hill, I just saw her,
like you!" My breast rejoiced, all my troubles over, she was
content, too old to care or yell her grudge, only complaining
her bad teeth. What long-sought peace!

Then glad of life I woke
in Boulder before dawn, my second story bedroom windows
Bluff Street facing East over town rooftops, I returned
from the Land of the Dead to living Poesy, and wrote
this tale of long lost joy, to have seen my mother again!
And when the ink ran out of my pen, and rosy violet
illumined city treetop skies above the Flatiron Front Range,
I went downstairs to the shady living room, where Peter Orlovsky
sat with long hair lit by television glow to watch
the sunrise weather news, I kissed him & filled my pen and wept.

October 5, 1983, 6:35 A.M.

Empire Air

Flying to Rochester Institute of Technology

Rising above the used car lots & colored dumps of Long Island
stubby white smokestreams drift North above th' Egyptic Factory
        roof'd monolith
into gray clouds, Conquer the world!
World Health restored with organic orange juice & Tibetan mule-dung-
        smelling Pills—Conquer the World Conquer the World
Conquer the World of Ego, Conquer World Anger
Conquer brick Worlds, Mortal Factories!
Conquer the Dewdrop? Conquer white clouded Sky we pass through?—
O ever-rising intelligent Sun conquer the night of Mind
Conquer War O Technologic Warrior
I ride above the Sun
                I look down into the Sun
I'm equal to Sun, Sun & I on the level
I've no appendicitis, I hang a Brooks Brothers tie
My clothes are Salvation Army! Conquer America! Conquer Greed!
        Conquer warmonger Hands!
Conquer yourself! Conquer your gluttony Ginsberg! Conquer lust for
        Conquest!
Conquer Conquest at last! All right Jack Number One! Creon wrecks
        Imperial City!
Conquer by Calm! Conquer by not getting laid, growing younger &
        older same time!
Conquer by having a hard on! Conquer all space by giving it away! Con-
        quer the Universe by inhabiting it!
Conquer by Dying! By eating decently! Wash yr behind after you move
        your bowels!
Pronounce your mother American language marvelously, mouth every
        syllable, savor every vowel, appreciate each consonant!
above the clouds! Conquer Karma, the chain of Cause and Effect
Conquer Cause & Effect, see it work the Cold War!
See it work in your heart!
Insult your girlfriend you'll feel hurt!
Insult Nicaragua you feel lousy
Insult the President you insult yourself
Conquer the President by not insulting him!
Don't insult yourself! stop insulting the Russians! stop insulting the
        enemy!

It costs $220800000000 a year to insult the enemy!
Conquer Underdeveloped Nation Hunger Debt! Conquer World Grief
Bank default! Go Conquer mortal Nuclear Waste!
Then go back Conquer your own heart!

January 30, 1984

Surprise Mind

How lucky we are to have windows!
       Glass is transparent!
I saw that boy in red bathingsuit
          walk down the street.

July 7, 1984, 8:30 A.M.

Student Love

The boy's fresh faced, 18, big smile
underwear hangs below his shorts, he's a kid
                              still growing
legs strong, he hugs me, steps away—
In twenty years thick bellied,
      bright eyes dulled with office work,
    his children'll pout in the
                    bathroom—
Better get in bed with him on top of me now
        laughing at my pot belly
before decades pass, bring our bony skulls whispering
                    to the hospital bedside.

July 31, 1984

The Question

When that dress-gray, gray haired and gray-faced
goblin took charge of me then inside the gate,
which closed behind me for a couple years,
I was still cheerful exceedingly
cheerful nodding out (hadn't slept for days),
cheerful because taking part in real life
action again, two serious gentlemen
at my shoulders in a night-colored car which
special for me rolled across December's bridge,
cheerful because I'd yelled out in the street
that this one and that one should be notified,
cheerful because I thought the adventure
a minor excursion, but cheerful also,
because such a gray such a small Uncle
I'd never seen yet, he however
wasn't cheerful, was reassuringly
bored bananas, boringly signed for
my delivery and boringly
turned my seven pockets inside out,
then with a wooden face confiscated
handkerchief, pocketknife, bunch of keys,
next indifferently requested my belt
and examined personally whether
my underpants operated with string,
yawned apathetic patting me down,
last nearly napping asked for the laces
that wagged lighthearted from my shoetops—
"I can't walk like this"—he shrugged a shoulder.
Left hand holding my pants up, spellbound by
this unprecedented situation, yet
still cavalier I bowed deep presenting
him with the shoelaces in my right hand.
"What's the point anyhow? I really don't
intend to hang myself"—I assured him
lighthearted. "You don't?" he questioned. . . . "Why not?"
On his sallow face neither mockery nor hate.
That was when the fear caught up with me.

István Eörsi
Translated with author by A. G. September 5, 1984

In My Kitchen in New York

for Bataan Faigao

Bend knees, shift weight—
Picasso's blue deathhead self portrait
    tacked on refrigerator door—
This is the only space in the apartment
    big enough to do T'ai chi—
Straighten right foot & rise—I wonder
    if I should have set aside that garbage
    pail—
Raise up my hands & bring them back to
    shoulders—The towels and pajama
    laundry's hanging on a rope in the hall—
Push down & grasp the sparrow's tail—
    Those paper boxes of grocery bags are
    blocking the closed door—
Turn north—I should hang up all
    those pots on the stovetop—
Am I holding the world right?—That
    Hopi picture on the wall shows
    rain & lightning bolt—
Turn right again—thru the door, God
    my office space, a mess of
    pictures & unanswered letters—
Left on my hips—Thank God Arthur Rimbaud's
    watching me from over the sink—
Single whip—piano's in the room, well
    Steven & Maria finally'll move to their
    own apartment next week! His pants're
    still here & Julius in his bed—
This gesture's the opposite of St. Francis
    in Ecstasy by Bellini—hands
    down for me—
I better concentrate on what I'm doing—
    weight in belly, move from hips—
No, that was the single whip—that apron's
    hanging on the North wall a year
    I haven't used it once
Except to wipe my hands—the Crane

spreads its wings—have I paid
the electric bill?
Playing the guitar—do I have enough $
to leave the rent paid while I'm
in China?
Brush knee—that was good
halvah, pounded sesame seed,
in the icebox a week—
Withdraw & push—I should
get a loft or giant living room—
The land speculators bought up all
the square feet in Manhattan,
beginning with the Indians—
Cross hands—I should write
a letter to the *Times* saying
it's unethical.

Come to rest hands down knees
straight—I wonder how
my liver's doing. O.K. I guess
tonite, I quit smoking last
week. I wonder if they'll blow
up an H Bomb? Probably not.

Manhattan Midnight, September 5, 1984

It's All So Brief

I've got to give up
Books, checks, letters
File cabinets, apartment
pillows, bodies and skin
even the ache in my teeth.

September 14, 1984

I Love Old Whitman So

Youthful, caressing, boisterous, tender
Middle aged thoughtful, ten thousand noticings of shore ship or street,
workbench, forest, household or office, opera—
that conning his paper book again to read aloud to those few Chinese
        boys & girls
who know enough American tongue to ear his hand—
loath to select one leaf from another, loath to reject a sympathetic page
—the tavern boy's look, a stone prisoner's mustache-sweat, prostitute in
        the sun, garrulous old man waving goodbye on the stoop—
I skim *Leaves* beginning to end, this year in the Middle Kingdom
marvel his swimmers huffing naked on the wave
and touched by his desperado farewell, "Who touches this book touches
        a man"
tip the hat on my skull
to the old soldier, old sailor, old writer, old homosexual, old Christ poet
        journeyman,
inspired in middle age to chaunt Eternity in Manhattan,
and see the speckled snake & swelling orb earth vanish
after green seasons Civil War and years of snow
white hair.

                                        Baoding, China, November 20, 1984

Written in My Dream by W. C. Williams

"As Is
you're bearing

a common
Truth

Commonly known
as desire

No need
to dress

it up
as beauty

No need
to distort

what's not
standard

to be
understandable.

Pick your
nose

eyes ears
tongue

sex and
brain

to show
the populace

Take your
chances

on
your accuracy

Listen to
yourself

talk to
yourself

and others
will also

gladly
relieved

of the burden—
their own

thought
and grief.

What began
as desire

will end
wiser."
                    Baoding, November 23, 1984

One Morning I Took a Walk in China

Students danced with wooden silvered swords, twirling on hard packed
        muddy earth
as I walked out Hebei University's concrete North Gate,
across the road a blue capped man sold fried sweet dough-sticks, brown
        as new boiled doughnuts
in the gray light of sky, past poplar tree trunks, white washed cylinders
        topped
with red band the height of a boy—Children with school satchels sang
        & walked past me
Donkeys in the road, one big one dwarf pulling ahead of his brother,
        hauled a cart of white stones
another donkey dragged a load of bricks, other baskets of dirt—
Under trees at the crossing, vendors set out carts and tables of cigarettes,
mandarin Tangerines, yellow round pears taste crunchy lemony strange,
apples yellow red-pinked, short bananas half black'd green,
few bunches of red grapes—and trays of peanuts, glazed thumbsized
        crab-apples 6 on a stick,
soft wrinkled yellow persimmons sat dozens spread on a cloth in wet
        mud by the curb—
cookpots on charcoal near cornerside tables, noodle broth vegetables
        sprinkled on top
A white headed barber shook out his ragged towel, mirror hung on red
        nail in the brick wall
where a student sat, black hair clipped at ears straight across the back of
        his neck
Soft-formed gritty coal pellets lay drying on the sidewalk and down the
        factory alley, more black mats spread,
Long green cabbages heaped by the buildingside waiting for home pot,
        or stacked on hand-tractor carts the market verandah a few
        yards away—
Leeks in a pile, bright orange carrots thick & rare, green unripe tomatoes,
        parsley, thin celery stalks awful cheap, potatoes & fish—
little & big heads chopped or alive in a tub, tiny fresh babies or aged carp
        in baskets—
a half pig on a slab, two trotters stick out, a white burlap shroud covered
        his body cleaved in half—
meat of the ox going thru a grinder, white fat red muscle & sinew
        together squeezed into human spaghetti—

Bicycles lined up along the concrete walk, trucks pull in & move out
      delivering cows dead and fresh green-stalked salad—
Downstreet, the dry-goods door—soap, pencils, notebooks, tea, fur coats
      lying on a counter—
Strawberry jam in rusty-iron topped jars, milk powder, dry cookies with
      sweetmeats
inside dissolve on the tongue to wash down fragrant black tea—
Ah, the machine shop gateway, brick walled latrine inside the truck yard
      —enter, squat on a brick & discharge your earth
or stand & pee in the big hole filled with pale brown squishy droppings
      an hour before—
Out, down the alleyway across the street a factory's giant smokestack,
      black cloud-fumes boiling into sky
gray white with mist I couldn't see that chimney a block away, coming
      home
past women on bicycles heading downtown their noses & mouths covered
      with white cotton masks.

Baoding, November 23, 1984, 9:30 P.M.

Reading Bai Juyi

I

I'm a traveler in a strange country
China and I've been to many cities
Now I'm back in Shanghai, days
under warm covers in a room with electric heat—
a rare commodity in this country—
hundreds of millions shiver in the north
students rise at dawn and run around the soccerfield
Workmen sing songs in the dark to keep themselves warm
while I sleep late, smoke too much cough,
turn over in bed on my right side
pull the heavy quilt over my nose and go back
to visit the dead my father, mother and immortal
friends in dreams. Supper's served me,
I can go out and banquet, but prefer
this week to stay in my room, recovering
a cough. I don't have to sell persimmons on the streetcurb
in Baoding like the lady with white bandanna'd head
Don't have to push my boat oars around a rocky corner
in the Yangtze gorges, or pole my way downstream
from Yichang through yellow industrial scum, or carry water
buckets on a bamboo pole over my shoulder
to a cabbage field near Wuxi—I'm famous,
my poems have done some men good
and a few women ill, perhaps the good
outweighs the bad, I'll never know.
Still I feel guilty I haven't done more;
True I praised the dharma from nation to nation
But my own practice has been amateur, seedy
—even I dream how bad a student I am—
My teacher's tried to help me, but I seem
to be lazy and have taken advantage of money
and clothes my work's brought me, today
I'll stay in bed again & read old Chinese poets—
I don't believe in an afterworld of god or even
another life separate from this incarnation
Still I worry I'll be punished for my carelessness
after I'm dead—my poems scattered and my name

forgotten and my self reborn a foolish workman
freezing and breaking rocks on a roadside in Hebei.

Shanghai, December 5, 1984, 10 A.M.

I I

"Ignorant and contentious" I spent lunch
arguing about boys making love with a student.
Still coughing, reclusive, I went back to bed
with a headache, despite afternoon sun
streaming through the French windows
weakly, to write down these thoughts.
Why've I wanted to appear heroic, why
strain to accomplish what no mortal could—
Heaven on earth, self perfection, household
security, & the accomplishment of changing the World.
A noble ambition, but that of a pathetic dreamer.
Tomorrow if I recover from bronchitis
I'll put on a serious face and go down to the Market.

2:30 P.M.

III

Lying head on pillow aching
still reading poems of Tang roads
Something Bai said made me press my finger
to my eyes and weep—maybe his love
for an old poet friend, for I also
have gray on my cheek and bald head
and the Agricultural poet's in the madhouse this week
a telegram told me, more historical
jackanapes maybe tragic maybe comic
I'll know when I come home around the world.
Still with heavy heart and aching head I read on
till suddenly a cry from the garden reminded me
of a chicken, head chopped off running circles spurting blood
from its neck on farm yard dirt, I was eleven years old,
or the raptured scream of a rabbit—I put down my book
and listened carefully to the cry almost drowned
by the metal sound of cars and horns—It was a bird
repeating its ascending whistle, pipe notes burst
into a burble of joyful tones ending wildly
with variable trills in swift succession high and low
and high again. At least it wasn't me, not my song,
a sound outside my mind, nothing to do with my aching brow.

3:30 P.M.

IV

I lay my cheek on the pillow to nap
and my thoughts floated against the stream
up to Zhong Xian west of the Three Gorges
where Bai Juyi was Governor.
"Two streams float together and meet further on
and mingle their water. Two birds fly upward
beneath the ninth month's cold white cloud.
Two trees stand together bare branched
rooted in the same soil secretly touching.
Two apples hung from the same bough last
month and disappeared into the Market."
So flowed my mind like the river, like the wind.
"Two thoughts have risen together in dream therefore
Two worlds will be one if I wake and write."
So I lifted my head from my pillow and Woke
to find I was a sick guest in a vast poor kingdom
A famous visitor honored with a heated room,
medicines, special foods and learned visitors
inquiring when I'd be well enough to lecture my hosts
on the musics and poetics of the wealthy
Nation I had come from half way round the world

8:15 P.M.

I sat up in bed and pondered what I'd learned
while I lay sick almost a month:
That monks who could convert Waste to Treasure
were no longer to be found among the millions
in the province of Hebei. That *The Secret of the Golden Lotus*
has been replaced by the Literature of the Scar, nor's hardly
anybody heard of the *Meditation Cushion of the Flesh*
That smoking Chinese or American cigarettes makes me cough;
Old men had got white haired and bald before
my beard showed the signs of its fifty-eight snows.
That of Three Gorges on the Yangtze the last one downstream
is a hairpin turn between thousand-foot-high rock mountain gates.
I learned that the Great Leap Forward caused millions
of families to starve, that the Anti-Rightist Campaign
against bourgeois "Stinkers" sent revolutionary poets
to shovel shit in Xinjiang Province a decade before
the Cultural Revolution drove countless millions of readers
to cold huts and starvation in the countryside Northwest.
That sensitive poetry girls in Shanghai dream
of aged stars from Los Angeles movies. That down the alley
from the stone bridge at Suzhou where Jiang Ji spent
a sleepless night wakened by the bell of Cold Mountain Temple,
water lapping against his boat a thousand years ago,
a teahouse stands with two-stringed violin and flutes
and wooden stage. That the gold in the Sun setting
at West Lake Hangzhou is manufactured from black Soft Coal.
That roast red-skinned juicy entire dogs with eyes
bulging from their foreheads hang in the market at Canton
That So-Chan meditation's frowned on and martial health
Qi-Gong's approved by Marxist theoreticians. That men in
deep-blue suits might be kind enough to file a report
to your Unit on gossip they've heard about your secret loves.
That "Hang yu hang yu!" song is heard when workmen labor
yodeling on bamboo scaffolds over the street outside all night.
That most people have thought "We're just little men,
what can we count" since the time of Qin Shi Huang.

VI

Tho the body's heavy meat's sustained
on our impalpable breath, materialists
argue that Means of Production cause History:
once in power, materialists argue what
the right material is, quarrel with each other,
jail each other and exile tens of millions
of people with 10,000 thoughts apiece.
They're worse than Daoists who quibbled about immortality.
Their saving grace this year's that all the peasants are fed.

VII   Transformation of Bai's "*A Night in Xingyang*"

I grew up in Paterson New Jersey and was
just a virginal kid when I left
forty years ago. Now I'm around the world,
but I did go back recently to visit my stepmother.
Then I was 16 years old, now I'm fifty eight—
All the fears I had in those days—I can still see myself
daydreaming reading N.Y. Times on the Chinese rug on the living room
floor on Graham avenue. My childhood houses are torn down,
none of my old family lives here any more,
mother under the ground in Long Island, father underground
near the border of Newark where he was born.
A highway cuts thru the Fair Street lot where I remember our earliest
apartment, & a little girl's first kiss. New buildings rise on that street,
all the old stores along Broadway have disappeared.
Only the Great Falls and the Passaic river flow
noisy with mist then quietly along the brick factory sides
as they did before.

10:15 P.M.

After Rewi Alley's *Bai Juyi, 200 Selected Poems* (Beijing: New World Press, 1983), p. 303.

Black Shroud

Kunming Hotel, I vomited greasy chicken sandwiched
in moldy bread, on my knees before the white toilet
retching, a wave of nausea, bowels and bladder loose
black on the bathroom floor like my mother groaning
in Paterson 1937. I went back to bed
on the twelfth floor, city lights twinkling north,
Orion in his belt bright in the sky, I slept again.

She had come into the bathroom her face hidden
in her breast, hair overhanging her figure bent in front
of me, stiff in hypertension, rigor mortis
convulsed her living body while she screamed
at the doctor and apartment house we inhabited.
Some electric current flowing up her spine tortured her,
foot to scalp unbearable, some professional advice
required quick action, I took her wrists, and held her
bound to the sink, beheading her silently with swift
dispatch, one gesture, a stroke of the knife-like ax
that cut thru her neck like soft thick gum, dead quick.

What had I done, and why? Certainly her visage
showed the reason, strain and fright lasting thru death.
But couldn't leave her body hidden in the toilet, someone
finding her bent over might wait, then push, then
horrified find her headless, skull fallen to the floor.
I picked her up by the shoulders, afraid to look at
the Medusa head
                which I lifted by long hair & set
on the sink before the mirror, but beheld no mad
drawn-cheek wild-eyed or blood-splotched wrinkled forehead—
Calm, beautiful face, tranquil in life's last moments
as if in prayer, eyes clear and modest, face content
with neither smile or frown but even-browed, eyebrows
in repose, cheeks colored healthy still as when alive.
"I made a mistake" I thought, in following the doctors' rules,
or where'd I get th' idea she was screaming and banging
her head on the wall in neural agony? Was that just my thought
or hadn't others told me so? Why'd I do it so abrupt
without consulting the World or the rest of the family—

Her look at last so tranquil and true made me wonder
why I'd covered her so early with black shroud.
Had I been insane myself and hasty? I left the room.

At Joel the doctor's wedding party the family'd gathered
whoever was left alive. Yes of course they found her corpse,
they knew she was crazy, but didn't announce a murder,
just whispered among themselves she was dead in the bathroom
causes unknown, tho headless, hard for her to suicide herself,
a further investigation would clarify this big mistake.
In fact my cousin my publisher with troubled frown
put the matter to rest, saying he'd call on the police
after the wedding guests go home. I said—
"I might be able to clear up the mystery. You saw
her head?" He looked at me surprised, how did I know
she was dead with her head cut off? I realized
I'd given myself away, but risked it, why lie more,
build up Karma nightmare another year & then get caught?
Police find my fingerprints on Naomi's dead neck? or my blade
be found under my bed, in the dust behind the refrigerator
on East 12th Street Lower East Side, I be arrested
in newspaper scandal? "You saw the head?" I asked
again, giving my knowledge away. "But are you sure?"
he asked. Dressed in his Harvard suit and silken tie
striped red and gold, "We have our legal staff, perhaps you should
consult with them, no fee, fortunate contract,
our clients we value, you for your Collected Works we do
protect without question." Helpful, alas, too late for me
to undo the murder of my mother, I must confess, I had
confessed, too late to undo confession and truth, I woke.

                                        December 21, 1984, 5:12 A.M.

World Karma

China be China, B.C. Clay armies underground the First Han Emperor's
        improvement
on burying his armies alive
Later Ming tombs buried excavator architects
& Mao officially buried 20,000,000 in Shit Freeze & Exile, much Suicide
especially bilingual sophisticates in the molecular structure of surfaces,
        machine-tool engineers
and Poetic intelligentsia questioned his Imperial vision of Pure Land
        future communist afterworld

Russia had Czars & Stalin, all Yiddish Poets shot August 12, 1952 in
        Lubyanka basement, everybody got drunk afterward,
everyone still whispers on streetcorners

America forever democratic, lawless sheriffs shot Indians, bad men, good
        men, chinks kikes niggers and each other

Spain always killed bulls & loved blood, matadors & crucifixion, reds &
        fascists assassinated anarchists—

The Jews always complained, kvetching about false gods, and erected the
        biggest false God, Jehovah, in middle of western civilization—
For creating the Judge the Jews are judged that's their world Karma
        continuing, the Atom bomb

British always had sense of superiority, class, stiff upperlip, the Queen
        and fuck you ducky up your bloody 'ole

The French, advanced sense of superiority, stiff back, Algérie is always
        indissolubly a part of La France,
We will not regret the necessity to kill you or anyone who disagrees
They appreciate everything wine women song modern art
O la la they're so smart, introduced opium cultivation
Indochina will always be an indissoluble addiction to France, the Bourse

Germans had Kaisers Hitlers, orderly meticulous and rational a bunch of
        beasts
now want Nuclear arms They're also intelligent Pride themselves on
        Science

romantic Poetry, their Black Forest mysterious full of Solitude acid rain
hi tech civilization First the ovens of Auschwitz now goodbye ancient
       trees
we have to keep up with the vulgar Americans

Italy the trains never ran on time, they got good shoes & Pope & Mafia
also good tomatoes and Angelico Beato, who'd want to complain in
       Naples or Uffizi?

In 200 years America'll have a billion people like neon China
Computerized students'll sleep six abed and hawk their mucus on the
       morning floor
before fighting to get into the shower—much less a piece of soap
and half stick of bacon with their petrochemical Wheaties & eggs—
       That's because
we had to Get Back to America, let's Stand Up Tall
so we can insult the rest of the world.

More!—The Moslems expansionist monotheists will go Jihad whenever
       able
Always their god best god only god only name Allah and
die like a dog if you don't believe me! From Morocco to Java
heathen dogs and cats go barking and meow after terrific Nobodaddy
in Paradise the Western lands Heaven Pure Land Garden of Sky,
other side of Eternal Dreamtime I vote for Australian Aborigines!
Let them run the world after Hi Tech's annihilated all other species &
       genetic strains
from whale to donkey sperm.

                   Kunming, *December 24, 1984, Midnight–12:49*

Prophecy

As I'm no longer young in life
and there seem to me not
so many pleasures to look forward to
How fortunate to be free
to write of cars and wars, truths of eras,
throw away old useless
ties and pants that don't fit.

January 9, 1985

Memory Cousins

After Long Absence, I returned from the land of the dead
to visit my stepmother in her suburban apartment.
I looked from a distance, was it a mental hospital
standing on a grass plain far from Manhattan's skyscrapers
after crossing Washington Bridge, or Jersey's tract houses
risen gigantic during my exile in China? I'd
been gone so long my relatives'd grown old at their doors—
a neighbor widow come out to empty the black plastic
garbagebag, I'd known her middle age, now with white hair
she gazed at me nodding absently, I'd not been gone long
while her husband'd died, children married with children now—
How dear to see me, where'd I been? I looked down the long hall,
door after door of Aunts and Uncles retired alive
white haired, television bound seeing the doctor, eating
delicatessen salad Sundays, reading best seller
books, dusting furniture, cleaning kitchen floors, happily
visiting Doctors for minor blood pressure, depression
or hernias. Years ahead, they should live so long, they'd die,
I'd never see them again, best settle down while childhood
memory cousins and brothers were old, but still alive,
enjoy each other's tables and coffee, business gossip.
Where else go off to, unhappy Russia warring Israel?
Here in America, peace, a place to live together.
They were bombing Nicaragua, factories exploding
in India, Cities crowded with Animal muggers
newspapers said, TV had pictures of them every nite—
Peter in fact just came back from Nuclear Buddhaland,
His belly exposed to Radiation a soft yellow
spot near his navel, he smiled rueful pulling his shirt
above his belt to show his mortal sore, what could cure him?
If go away now I'll be gone forever, Peter,
Stepmother Edith, Aunt Honey & Leo, Aunt Clara
and Uncle Abe, my brother Gene & Connie & the kids,
I may never see them again. Here are their living eyes,
here's the end of the Immortal Dream.

March 2, 1985, 7:56 A.M.

Moral Majority

Something evil about you Mr. Viguerie Mr. Falwell Robertson Swaggert.
Not evil but ignorance of the delights of the Boy
The 1920s have passed, corsets chastity belts whips
the stake, Lesbian cities aflame in your fiery eyes
—Some old Demon the Satan in possession of your body
a thousand years old, two thousand that burned the parchments of Black
        Sappho
I've seen God as much as any, he doesn't look like you alone
He looks like me too, all the homosexuals on earth,
in Congo, Cities of North America, Rio Barrios—
He looks like a lavender fairy, Paris salons 1890 the birds & bees,
Like an ambidextrous worm, male dogs coupling in the Alabama parking-
        lot.
Nothing wrong with Family, Mother Father & Buba.
Nothing wrong with the Babe.
Nothing wrong with Mr. Falwell except a little mean streak
that isn't god, just a jerk, talks too big for his britches,
inexperienced Bible Salesman
interprets words & letters, not Holy Spirit
ambitious politically, at the expense of the poor,
the thwarted, & happy ruddy kids—
Find out Buddha, enter the great silence
& pass thru the needle's eye,
then come back happy, laughing, generous
big mouth full of good cheer, not money,
honey.

March 19, 1985

The Guest

I've a pain in my back
Fifth lumbar & sacrum
Kidneystones alas alack
can't drink milk calcium
High blood pressure about
salt I can't eat
at my age no red meat
sometimes I get gout

My age fifty eight
My friend Peter's away
I should lose ten pounds weight
Prostrate every day
to my guru who's Crazy
Prepare for grim death
Exercise for good health
All my life I've been lazy

Little gold, lots of fame
Small flat in Manhattan
tho I bank on my name
my wallet won't fatten
But the thing I want most
to embody my joy
is the belly of a boy
and there I get lost

I met David he undressed
Came naked on my bed
He climbed on my chest
"I love you Allen" he said
He touched and caressed
my stomach, heart and thigh
appreciated my sigh
I slept chaste & blessed.

He visited New York
to sleep a week in my room
watch me at work,

enlighten my gloom—
Body young & strong
shapely from Basketball
Skin muscular stomach small
"I can't be your lover long."

Mind tender, he loves girls
Sees me as poetry master
His pubic hair's soft curls
press my breast to rapture
His smooth cock grows thick
my heart beats at his loin
He presses with his groin
His hands caress my neck

I touch around his buttocks
smooth, firm and warm.
"I've never been fucked"
he encourages, as my arm
reaches up his spine
passes down his back
presses into his open crack
He turns on his belly to try.

I enter slow, he's soft
no pain, he raises his behind
no hard on, hips aloft
I push, he doesn't mind.
My trouble is, I'm old
and tho this young kind boy
gives me a chance for joy
I'm not hard enough to be bold.

Yet I'm in, "How does it feel now?"
"It's O.K., it's kind of different."
Ruddy face, eyes open on the pillow,
he lies before me prone, no effort—
I'm afraid to move, what'll he say?
But he humps his rear up more
to take what's in store,
I stick it in all the way.

Something is missing my hard on
But it's what I have, it works
I pump him slowly, then start on
moving faster while he jerks
his buttocks up to help me come,
I ask permission, he says "yes,"
I pull his hips up, hold his breast,
spurt my loves deep in his bum

Next night we hugged and slept
Chaste again and affectionate
I answered the phone all day but kept
winding him in my mental net—
He wasn't excited by my body
I couldn't expect his sexual love
After this week would I approve
his visiting, if I had to sleep lonely?

March 24, 1985

After Antipater

I've climbed the Great Wall's stone steep out of breath
sat on gray columns broken at Acropolis' marble sill
brushed past morbid scented insect eating plants in Petén Rainforest
Eaten roastbeef with my mother's cousins atop a World Trade Tower
  overhanging Hudson River
Slept under the dome echoing lament for Mumtaz Mahal's white skull
Stood in Red Square snow across from the Kremlin wall-tomb of th'-
  assassin of millions
Climbed Seville's gypsy balconies, Sagrada Familia's crannied spires,
  gazed through my father's eyes from San Marco's high porch
tarried on Brooklyn bridge facing Manhattan dusk's sparkling Towers,
  walked Golden Gate's Pacific promenade
But when you lay on my bed, white sheet covering your loins, your eyes
  on mine
I forgot these marvels, my heart breathed open, I saw life's glory look
  back at me naked.

March 26, 1985

Greek Anthology III, Book IX, Epigram 58, Loeb, p. 31.

Jumping the Gun on the Sun

Sincerity
is the key
to living
in Eternity

If you love
Heav'n above
Hold your ground,
Look around
Hear the sound
of television,
No derision,
Smell your blood
taste your good
bagels & lox
Wash your sox
& touch wood,
It's understood
This is it
wild wit
Make your love
on earth above,
home of the brave,
Save yr grave
for future days
Present here
nothing to fear
No need to sigh
no need to die
before your time
mentally whine
stupidly dine
on your own meat
That's what's neat
Mortally great
Immortally sweet
Incredibly deep
makes you weep
Just this once

Don't be a dunce
Take your cap
off Hear my rap

Sincerity
is the key
to living in
Eternity

Makes you wise
in your own eyes
makes the body
not seem shoddy
Makes your soul
completely whole
empty, final
indefinable
Mobile, total-
ly undeniable
Affirmative action
for no faction
for all men
women too,
mother brother,
even for you
Dead soul'd, sick
but really quick
with breath & thick
with blood in yr prick
Walking alive
on Riverside Drive
up on Broadway
shining gay
in New York
waving you dork
waving your mind
or living behind
your meaty masque
magnificent task
all you could ask
as if pure space
gave you a place

in Eternity—
To see the City
Stand all day
Shine all night
Bright starlight
streaming the height
Watery lawn
misty at dawn
warmed by the sun
Bathed in the moon
green grasses of June
80 times only
Don't be lonely
Roses are live
Cockroaches thrive
in plastic garbage
maggots salvage
your dead meat
Horses eat
golden Hay
in golden day
Young kids jump
in the City dump
Take the lump
in your throat
and sing out
yr holy note
of heart's delight
in living light
Day & Night

*Sincerity
is the key
to Bliss in this
Eternity*

                    April 5, 1985

Cadillac Squawk

Sitting on the twelfth floor Gomden I heard a wild siren in the garment
        district
Heard dog scream at dog on park avenue
my head rumbled the Bronx 242'd street Lexington Avenue Express
lonesome sparrows chirped weathered coppergreen cornice 1860
Footstep crash, pocket change jangled the shrine room's polished floor
traffic waves rushed the shore 1985
Adolf Hitler's voice in the taxi horn
squeak soprano steely cheep Chevrolet brakeshafts
subway breath rising to Empire State Observation Roof
iron doors slam refrigerators shut
bones creak in my knees' antechambers
Heard the long Cadillac horn squawk up sidestreet brick buildingsides
elevators ascended and descended a thousand skyscrapers
wheels within wheels rubber and steel revolve on asphalt corridors
Exhaust puffs out monoxide Broadway Manhattan
Heard the sky shut up
Heard conversation in the trees in leafy Bronx
Heard Africa sigh
Asia turned over in its sleepy bunk
blood ran down rocks in South America
Heard Central America squeeze its ribs through iron gates
the Middle East rumbled plates & spoons in wartime bomb rubble
Polynesians danced with bacteria
Heard Japonesia eat with chopsticks chewing rice & peapods
Heard Australia rattle song sticks singing in Simpson Desert after the end
        of the world

New York Dharmadatu, June 16, 1985, 3:33 P.M.

Things I Don't Know

Dawn, a mastiff howls on the porch across the street behind the For Sale
signed tree
Chatter Chirp Chirp Chatter Chirp Chir Chir Chic Chir chance birdie
twitters in a maple tree branch, Twirp!
I wake, what bird's that, what kind of dog moans so?
Is that a maple or an oak, on Mapleton Street? What flowers weeds &
ferns, those in the backyard? What car goes by awhoosh? A Pontiac,
swash up the street,
A Chevy, Ford, a Pinto, a Grammarian, a 4 wheel drive GM?
What star I saw last night when clouds lifted & Orion's belt
Glittered gold on blue? or was that amber on azure? As my eye
followed his arrow past the North Star thru the void, was that a tiny
galaxy shimmering?
Where's Sagittarius, which way is the black hole at center of the Spiral
Nebula?
Where's Sahel where a million children starve? Where's Libya where
Wilson of the CIA trained terrorists?
How many times this century'd the Marines land on Nicaragua's dirty
flag?
Who killed Roque Dalton? What's the size of U.S. national Debt?
& how much interest we pay each year till the Eighties end?
Now the bird's quiet & the dog bark's down, what's differential calculus?
How do you fix electric socket wires?
I used to know the names of all the minerals. I do remember Pectolite
gave you like asbestos splinters.
How do people overcome panic driving cars? Are bird bones hollow?
didn't I once know the look of grackle & scarlet tanager?
Cirrus or cumulus, what cloud produces thunder, lightning, rain?
What makes electricity in a battery? How does my wind charger friction
become electric?
When water pours into hydraulic ram, what makes it squirt uphill when
the valve closes in the Pressure Chamber? Is that it? Something like
that?
What're the 12 pix in Conditioned Co-existent Emergence's Chain?
Blind man, potter, monkey tree, boat world, house with seven windows,
what comes next before the man with arrow in his eye?
What about banks? What's common stock & preferred? What's a fu-
tures?
How do you hang a door, frame a window? Hold a light chainsaw?

How fix a broken leg? Ease a heart attack, deliver a baby? Breathe in
    the mouth of a man dying at oceanside?
What kind of government ever worked? Who wrote English Choriam-
    bics?
This isn't Trivia (how play that?) this is my life, I can't remember
the name of the lawyer my fellow student, friends with me in college 40
    years ago—
How make a living, if I couldn't write poetry?
Would I know how to plant peas, tie up tomato stalks?

July 21, 1985

Index of Titles and First Lines
(*Titles are in italics.*)